10086 →

SUNSET BLVD.

VOCAL SELECTIONS

MUSIC BY

ANDREW LLOYD WEBBER

LYRICS BY

DON BLACK & CHRISTOPHER HAMPTON

A REALLY USEFUL GROUP PUBLICATION

ANDREW LLOYD WEBBER

COMPOSER / PRODUCER

Andrew Lloyd Webber was born in 1948. He is the composer of *Joseph and the Amazing Technicolor Dreamcoat*, *Jesus Christ Superstar*, the film scores of *Gumshoe*, and *The Odessa File*, *Jeeves*, *Evita*, *Variations* and *Tell Me on a Sunday* combined as *Song & Dance*, *Cats*, *Starlight Express*, *Requiem*, a setting of the Latin Requiem Mass, *The Phantom of the Opera*, *Aspects of Love* and *Sunset Boulevard*.

His awards include four Tony Awards, four Drama Desk Awards, three Grammys, including the award for Best Classical Contemporary Composition for *Requiem* in 1986, and five Laurence Olivier Awards.

He is the first person to have three musicals running in New York and three in London, a record achieved in 1982, 1988 and again in 1994. He is the first recipient of the American Society of Composers, Authors and Publishers' Triple Play Award.

Andrew Lloyd Webber, through The Really Useful Group, produces not only his own, but other writers' works including *Shirley Valentine*, *Lend Me a Tenor*, *La Bête* and his revival of *Joseph and the Amazing Technicolor Dreamcoat*.

In 1988 he was awarded Fellowship of the Royal College of Music.

In 1992 he was awarded a knighthood for his services to the arts and in February 1993 he was given a Star on the Hollywood Walk of Fame.

DON BLACK

BOOK & LYRICS

Sunset Boulevard marks Don Black's third theatrical collaboration with Andrew Lloyd Webber. They first joined forces to write the song cycle *Tell Me on a Sunday*. This was developed to form the basis of the stage show *Song & Dance*. They were reunited (together with Charles Hart) for *Aspects of Love*.

Other songs they have written together include the Olympic Games theme *Amigos Para Siempre* for Sarah Brightman and José Carreras and *Next Time You Fall In Love*, the love duet for the re-vamped *Starlight Express*.

Don made his West End début as a lyricist with composer John Barry on the musical *Billy*, starring Michael Crawford (Theatre Royal, Drury Lane).

In a career that has won him many glittering prizes (an Oscar, five Academy Award nominations, three Tony nominations, a Golden Globe, five Ivor Novello Awards and many platinum, gold and silver discs) he has worked with some of the world's leading composers - Jule Styne, Henry Mancini, Elmer Bernstein, Quincy Jones and Charles Strouse.

Amongst Don's many popular songs are: *Ben*, a number one for Michael Jackson; *To Sir With Love*, an American number one for Lulu; *Born Free*; a trio of James Bond title songs - *Thunderball*, *Diamonds are Forever* and *The Man with the Golden Gun*; *Walk Away* (his first hit sung by Matt Monro); *True Grit* (Glen Campbell); *I'll Put You Together Again* (Hot Chocolate); *Take That Look Off Your Face* (Marti Webb); and *Love Changes Everything* (Michael Ball).

Don started out as a stand-up comedian and blames himself entirely for the death of Variety.

He is vice-president of the British Academy of Songwriters, Composers and Authors and chairman of the Vivian Ellis Prize, an annual event founded to encourage young people to write for the musical theatre.

CHRISTOPHER HAMPTON

BOOK & LYRICS

Christopher Hampton was born in Fayal in the Azores in 1946. He graduated in Modern Languages from New College, Oxford in 1968 and from 1968 to 1970 he was the resident dramatist at the Royal Court.

Plays: *When Did You Last See My Mother?* (1966); *Total Eclipse* (1968); *The Philanthropist* (1970); *Savages* (1973); *Treats* (1976); *The Portage to San Christobal of A.H.* (from the novel by George Steiner - 1982); *Tales from Hollywood* (1982); *Les Liaisons Dangereuses* (from the novel by Laclos - 1985); *White Chameleon* (1990).

Television: *Able's Will* (1977); *The History Man* (from the novel by Malcolm Bradbury - 1981); *The Price of Tea* (1984); *Hotel du Lac* (from the novel by Anita Brookner - 1986); *The Ginger Tree* (from the novel by Oswald Wynd - 1989).

Film: *A Doll's House* (1973); *Tales from the Vienna Woods* (1979); *The Honorary Consul* (1983); *The Good Father* (1986); *Wolf at the Door* (1986); *Dangerous Liaisons* (1988).

Translations: Four plays by Ibsen; two plays by Molière; three plays by Ödön von Horváth; Chekhov's *Uncle Vanya*.

Awards: The *Evening Standard* Award on three occasions (*The Philanthropist* - 1970, *Tales from Hollywood* - 1983 and *Les Liaisons Dangereuses* - 1986); *Plays and Players* London Theatre Critics' Award on three occasions (*The Philanthropist* - 1970, *Savages* - 1973 and *Les Liaisons Dangereuses* - 1985); the Los Angeles Drama Critics' Circle Award for *Savages* (1974); *Screen International* Award for *Tales from the Vienna Woods* (1980); the Laurence Olivier Award for *Les Liaisons Dangereuses* (1986); New York Drama Critics' Circle Award for *Les Liaisons Dangereuses* (1987); Prix Italia for *The Good Father* (1988); Writers' Guild Academy Award for *Dangerous Liaisons* (1988); Academy Award for *Dangerous Liaisons* (1988); a BAFTA Award for *Dangerous Liaisons* (1989).

INSPIRED BY SUNSET BOULEVARD

I first saw *Sunset Boulevard* sometime in the early 70s. It inspired a tune. This tune was supposed to be the title song. However, I neither had the rights to the film, nor at that time was likely to be able to obtain them. Eventually I used a couple of fragments of that tune in Stephen Frears' affectionate Bogart spoof, *Gumshoe*.

In 1976 Hal Prince began working with me on the musical *Evita*. We discussed *Sunset Boulevard* and I saw the movie again since Hal Prince had obtained the rights. It all came to nothing but I wrote an idea for the moment when Norma Desmond returns to Paramount Studios.

At around the same time I met with Christopher Hampton whom I had known for some years as he was at school with Tim Rice. He had already declared an interest in writing the libretto for the English National Opera of *Sunset Boulevard*, but this too had come to nothing. We thought it was a wonderful idea but came to the conclusion that in both our cases other projects made *Sunset* impossible and there was yet again the question of whether we would get the rights.

I thought of *Sunset* on and off over the next 12 years, but it was only after *Aspects of Love* that I felt it was the subject I had to compose next.

I contacted Paramount and, this time, the rights were available. So I took an option and started work. As ever, several early jottings were discarded. Then I had the idea of working with Chris Hampton once more. Chris was intrigued but felt that he would be happy working with somebody who had experience of lyrics before. I introduced him to my old friend and collaborator, Don Black, and what I hoped most would happen appears to have done so. They collaborated on both the book and lyrics together.

I began the score in 1989. The show opened at London's Adelphi Theatre on 12 July 1993. The Los Angeles production gave me and the whole creative team a chance to reconsider our first production. Just the presence of Billy Wilder and his incisive comments, which he generously gave, inspired us all.

ANDREW LLOYD WEBBER

LET'S HAVE LUNCH

MUSIC BY
ANDREW LLOYD WEBBER
LYRICS BY
DON BLACK & CHRISTOPHER HAMPTON

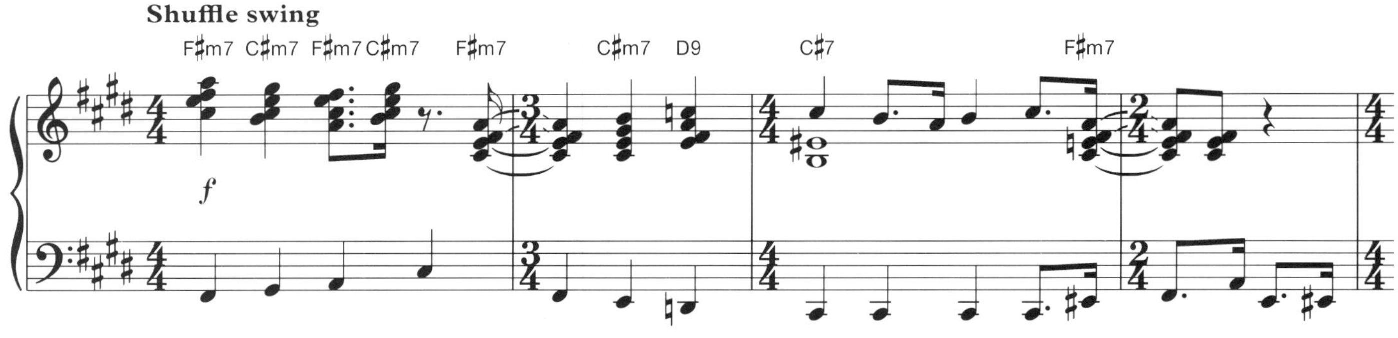

(JOE)
How can you work with Dar - ryl? Got - ta run, let's have lunch.
(MYRON)
shoot - ing a west - ern down at Fox.
We should talk, let's have lunch.
C♯m A7 G♯7
C♯m7 D♯m7 Em C♯m7 D♯m7 Em C♯m7 B2 A7
You look great.
MARY
Hi Mis - ter Gil - lis. I'm up for an au - di -
Dm B♭7/F A7

(JOE)
Shel - drake is dri - ving me in - sane.
(MARY)
- tion.
Dm
B♭7
We should talk, let's have lunch.
Don't for-get me when you're cast - ing. Got - ta run, let's have lunch.
A7
Dm
Em7 Dm(♭5)
Em6/C♯ F6/C
Fm6/C Em7/B B♭7
Morn - ing Jo-an - na.
JOANNA
Who are you meet - ing?
Hi there My - ron.
MYRON
You look great.
E♭m
E♭m(♭5)
C♭7

JOE
Shel-drake, but do I need it?
JOANNA
I'm hand - ing in my se - cond draft.
MARY
I've spent the last month fast-ing.
MYRON
I'm shoot-ing a west - ern down at Fox.
Bb7
Ebm
Ebdim
JOE
I'd real - ly love to read it.
MARY
Don't for-get me when you're cast - ing.
Ebm
B7
Bb7
JOANNA
We should talk.
JOE
Got - ta run.
MYRON
We should talk, got - ta run,
Ebm
Fm
Gbm
Ebm(b5)
Bb7
Gbm

Poco più mosso (not swing)
(JOE) + JOANNA
1st FINANCE MAN
Let's have lunch. We want the keys to your
(MYRON) + MARY
let's have lunch.
Ebm7 Db2/F Gbm G Cm
f
2nd FINANCE MAN
1st FINANCE MAN
car. You're way be - hind with the pay - ments. Don't give us
Ab Cm Fsus4 F Cm
Tempo primo
2nd FINANCE MAN
JOE
an - y fan - cy foot - work. Give us the keys. I
Abmaj7 Ab(b5) Abmaj7 D7b5

(JOE)
only wish I could help. I loaned it to my accountant. He has an important client down in Palm Springs. Felt like shooting the breeze.
1st FINANCE MAN
Are you telling us you walked here?
C♯m A C♯m
F♯ C♯m A Emaj7 B6/A C♯m7
E/A F♯m D♯m7(♭5)
G♯7 C♯m C♯m

Dialogue: 1st FINANCE MAN: "Or we're taking your car."
2nd FINANCE MAN: "We have a court order."
JOE: "I love it when you talk dirty."

JOE
That you Sam-my?
SAMMY
Bless you Jo - seph.
How do you like my ha - - rem?
Cm Dm7 G Cm Dm A♭7 G7 Cm
How come you get such lou - sy breaks?
Cm G Cm/A G Cm Dm E♭m
One learns to grin and bear 'em.
GIRLS
This is the
G7+ G7 Cm6 F7 G7 Cm7(♭5)/F

JOE
What - 're you play - ing?
(GIRLS)
big - gest film ev - er made.
F7 G7 Cm7(♭5) F7 G7 Cm Dm7
1ST GIRL
Tem - ple vir - gin.
2ND GIRL
Hand mai - den to De - li - lah . . .
Cm Dm E♭m G7+ G7 Cm6
JOE
Let's have lunch, got - ta run. You
Cm Dm E♭m Cm Dm E♭m Cm Dm/C A♭7/C A♭/C

got - ta find me a job. I'm
C♯m
A/C♯
way be - hind with my pay - ments. I thought you were
C♯m
F♯sus4
F♯
F♯/C♯
C♯m
meant to be my a - gent I need some work.
MORINO
I
Amaj7
Emaj7/A
Amaj7
D♯m7(♭5)
on - ly wish I could help. This town is dead at the mo -
Dm
B♭
Dm
Dm7

(MORINO)
- ment, there's been this slow down in pro -
G Dm B♭6 Fmaj7/B♭ B♭6(maj7) B♭6
JOE
- duc - tion. Who is this jerk?
Fmaj7/B♭ Em7♭5 A7 Dm
MORINO
He's my wun - der - kind from Broad - way. Ev - 'ry ma - jor
Dm B♭/D
stu - dio wants him play - ing one a - gainst the oth - er.
Dm/B B♭ Dm6 Gm7

JOE
What I need is three hun-dred bucks.
Gm6 A7 C♯m(♭5) D♯m Em C♯m(♭5) D♯m Em
C♯m(♭5) D♯m Em C♯m(♭5) D♯m Em C♯m D♯m E C♯m D♯m E
JOE ARTIE JOE
Hel - lo Ar - tie. Joe, you bas - tard. You ne - ver call me
Faug G7♭5 Faug F E
ARTIE
an - y more. Found a cu - ter dan - cing part - ner.
E Caug E7/B♭ E7/A♭ Eaug/G♭

(ARTIE)
How are things?
JOE
Not so great.
ARTIE
Will this help? Twen - ty bucks.
Am Bdim Cm Am Bdim Cm Am Bdim Cm Am Bdim Cm
mp
Am/G♭ Fdim Cm/E♭ Am/C Bdim Cm/A Am/C Bdim Cm/A A/G Dm/F Em
ff
SAMMY
Hi there Li - sa.
KATHERINE
I hate this wea - ther.
CLIFF
Where've you been hid-ing?
MARY
You look great. What're you do - ing?
MYRON
Mor - nin' Jo-an - na. How're you do - ing?
JOANNA
You look great.
LISA
R. K. O. are O. K.
GIRLS
This is the
Dm Am7 Dm7 Am7 Dm Am7 Dm7 Am7 Dm Em Fm Dm Em Fm

CLIFF
I'm trying to make my mind up.
SAMMY
They're talk - ing
MARY
Guess I was born to play her.
JOANNA
You look
DAWN
What is my mo - ti - va - tion?
(GIRLS)
big - gest film ev - er made.
A7
Dm
Dm
LISA
You should go work for War - ners.
ARTIE
We shoot next month. Got -
(SAMMY)
nom - in - a - tions.
TENORS
BARITONES
Got -
MYRON
Is your new script with Shel - drake?
Got -
(JOANNA)
great.
MORINO
I'm ve - ry close to Shel - drake.
(DAWN)
ADAM
Got -
A7
Dm
Em
Fm

(ARTIE)
- ta run.
KATHERINE
Let's have lunch. I've
(T.)
(B.)
- ta run.
MARY
It's bet - ween me and Die -
(MYRON)
- ta run.
JOANNA
Let's have lunch. I'm hand - ing in my se - cond
JOHN
Let's drive to Ve - gas this week - end?
(ADAM)
- ta run.
ANITA
You look great.
Dm Em Fm Dm C B♭7 A7
(KATHERINE)
land - ed a big Broad - way show.
ADAM + JOHN
I'm gon - na work for Me -
(MARY)
- trich.
(MARY)
Let's have
(JOANNA)
draft.
CLIFF
Let's have lunch.
MYRON
I'd_
GIRLS
Let's have lunch. This is the big - gest
B♭7 B♭7/A A7 B♭7

(ADAM + JOHN)
- tro.
JOHN
Let's have lunch. It won't work.
(MYRON)
LISA
— real-ly love to read — it. It won't work.
(MARY)
CLIFF
1st GROUP
lunch. I know just how to light you. We should talk.
MORINO
2nd GROUP
Let's pen-cil Thurs-day morn-ing. — Got - ta run.
(GIRLS)
film ev - er made.
B♭7 A7 B♭7 A7 B♭7 Gm6/A Dm6/A Fm6 Gm6/E Fm6/D Gm6/C Fm/B
TUTTI
S.
A.
Let's have lunch. Hi, good morn-ing. Aren't we luc-ky? Go-ing to work with Cu -
T.
B.
Fm6/B Gm6/A♭ Fm/G♭ Dm7 Dm B♭7 A7
f

rall.
a tempo
- kor. Par - a - mount is pa - ra - dise. Mo - vies from A to Zu -
Dm
Dm Am7 Dm7 Am7 Dm6 C9 B♭7/E A7
- kor. We should talk, got - ta run, let's have lunch! We
Dm7 Fm6/C Gm6/B♭ A♭m6 B♭7/A♭ Gm6 A♭m6/F Fm6 Gm6/E Ddim
JOE
should talk, got - ta run. Let's have lunch. Come to get your knife back?
A7

THE GREATEST STAR OF ALL

MUSIC BY
ANDREW LLOYD WEBBER
LYRICS BY
DON BLACK & CHRISTOPHER HAMPTON
WITH CONTRIBUTIONS BY AMY POWERS

E+ E E+ B7♭9 B9
sin - gle week she'd get ten thou - sand let - ters.
D C B♭
Men would of - fer for - tunes
E♭ B♭add 9 B♭
for a bloom from her cor - sage or a
Cm/B♭ F7/B♭ B♭ B7♭5
few strands from her hair. To -
mf
mp

E
Am6
E+
E
-day she's half for - got - ten,
E+
E
Am6/E
but it's the pic - tures that got small, she is the
A/B
B♭/B
B
E
great - est star of all.
F
B♭m6/F
F+
F
Then you can't i - ma - gine the way fans
mf

rubato
F+ F F+ B♭m/C C9
sa - cri - ficed them - selves to touch her sha - dow. There
a tempo
F B♭m/F F+ F
was a Mar - ha - ra - jah who hanged him -
F+ F F+ C7♭9 C9
- self with one of her dis - card - ed stock - ings.
E♭ D♭ C♭
She's im - mor - tal, caught in -

Fb/Cb
Cb
- side that flick - er - ing light beam is a
Fb/Gb
Gb7
Cb
C7b5
youth which can - not fade. Ma -
8va
loco
8va
f
F
Bbm/F
F+
F
F+
F
- dame's a liv - ing le - gend, I've seen so ma - ny i - dols
mf
Bbm6/F
Bb/C
B/C
C
F
Bbm/F
F+
F
fall, she is the great - est star of all.
rall.
mp
p

WITH ONE LOOK

MUSIC BY
ANDREW LLOYD WEBBER
LYRICS BY
DON BLACK & CHRISTOPHER HAMPTON
WITH CONTRIBUTIONS BY AMY POWERS

A/C♯ Em7 A D A/E E7 A
When I speak it's with my soul. I can play a-ny role. No
E7/A A E7/A D A/C♯ Bm7 E
words can tell the stor-ies my eyes tell. Watch me when I frown, you can't write that down. You
C G/C C G A F♯m7 A/E Bm7 E
know I'm right, it's there in black and white. When I look your way you'll hear what I say. Yes,
A F♯m Bm7 E E7/D
with one look I put words to shame, just one look sets the screen a-flame.

A/C♯ Em7 A D A/C♯ Bm7 E7
Si - lent mu-sic starts to play. One tear in my eye makes the whole world cry.
A F♯m Bm7 D/E E7/D
With one look they'll for - give the past, they'll re - joice I've re-turned at last
f
A/C♯ Em/B A/C♯ D A/E E7 A
to my peo-ple in the dark, still out there in the dark.
D Bm Em7 G/A A
f

D/F♯ Am D G D/F♯ Em7 A
Si - lent mu-sic starts to play. With one look you'll know all you need to know.
p
mf
B G♯m C♯m C♯m/B E/F♯ F♯/E
With one look I'll ig - nite a blaze, I'll re - turn to my glo - ry days.
B/D♯ F♯m7 B E2 E6
They'll say Nor-ma's back at last. This time I am stay-ing, I'm stay-ing for good, I'll be
rit.
molto rit.
a tempo
A Emaj7 E/F♯ B
back where I was born to be. With one look I'll be me.
ff

SURRENDER

MUSIC BY
ANDREW LLOYD WEBBER
LYRICS BY
DON BLACK & CHRISTOPHER HAMPTON

C(no 3rd) C F/C G/C
Here the tra-cers fly, light - ing up the sky,
p
C G/C F
but I'll fight on to the end.
Let them send their
L.H.
C/E B♭ E♭ G unison
ar - mies, I will ne-ver bend,
I won't see you now till I sur -
p
C G C
-ren - der,
I'll see you a - gain when I sur - ren - der.
8va

EVERY MOVIE'S A CIRCUS

MUSIC BY
ANDREW LLOYD WEBBER
LYRICS BY
DON BLACK & CHRISTOPHER HAMPTON

N.C. G D G D
SANDY MARY
What's wrong? Can't get a screen test, don't you hate it when a
A D D+ G C G
ALL JANE JOHN
yes man says no. Mo - vies. Good part? I'm a po - lice - man,
C G/B Am7 D7 G
GLYNN
'Hands up Punk,' that's all I say. First time I've
C G/B C G D7 G F D
ALL
worked on the lot there, I must say R. K. O. are O. K. Mo - vies.

SAMMY
KATE
G D G D
Then what? He pressed a but - ton, out of the wall fell a
A D
ALL
MYRON
JOANNA
G D
four - pos-ter bed. Mo - vies. Bu - sy? They shot my screen - play.
G D A D G
MYRON
JOANNA
ALL
Is - n't that great? No, they shot the thing dead. Ev - 'ry
C G C G Am7 D7 G F♯ G
mo - vie's a cir - cus, on the wire with - out a net.

(G) PETE C MICHELLE G C CLIFF G SASHA
Lone - ly? That's how I like it. Can't you be nice? Why we're
D7 G F ALL D ARTIE G D
not on the set. Mo - vies. Hey Joe, what are you slum - ming?
G JOE D A7 ARTIE D ALL JOE
Here for a meet - ing. This time of night? Mo - vies. It's some
G D G D A7 D F♯ ALL G
stu - di - o smart ass, you know I'm fa - mous for be - ing po - lite. Mo - vies.

ARTIE
Guess what?
C G
I'm get-ting mar - ried.
JOE
C G
Con - gra - tu - la - tions.
ARTIE
She'll
Am7 G
be right back.
F♯ G
ALL
Mo - vies.
ARTIE
Fact is
C G
we were just leav - ing,
C G
she's been stood up by some up - pi - ty hack.
D D7 G
F D
ALL
Mo - vies.
JOE
Mar - ried.
G D
Who would have thought it?
G D
Why don't you look hap - py,
A D
come on be brave.
F D
ALL
Mo - vies.

ARTIE
It's this_ mo - vie I'm shoot - ing._
JOE
You first as - sis - tant?
ARTIE
More like a slave!
ALL
Ev - 'ry_ mo - vie's a cir - cus,
ARTIE
but this is a cir - cus mov - ie as well.
ALL
Mo - vies.
ARTIE
Prob - lems, no - thing but prob - lems, a - ni - mals, ac - tors, two kinds of hell.
G D G D A7 D G C G C G/B Am7 D7 G F♯ G C G C G/D D7 G F D

G C G C G
ALL
Ev - 'ry mo - vie's a cir - cus, on the wire with -
Am7 D7 G F D G D
BETTY
- out a net._ Well hel - lo Mis-ter Gill - is.__
G/D D A7 D
ARTIE JOE ARTIE
You two have met? I'm the up - pi - ty hack. And she's______ the
G/D D G D A7 D
BETTY BARMAN
stu - di - o smart ass?_ What's go-ing on__ here? They're call - ing you back.

G C/G G C/G G
BETTY
I just_ re - read 'Blind Win - dows,' it needs some real re -
D7 G C/G G
- work - ing of course. If we_ fixed up the ope - ning,
C G/B D7 G
ARTIE
call up the wran - gler and pay off the horse.
ALL
Ev - 'ry_
C G C G/B Am7 D7 G
mo - vie's a cir - cus, on the wire with - out a net.

GIRL MEETS BOY

MUSIC BY
ANDREW LLOYD WEBBER
LYRICS BY
DON BLACK & CHRISTOPHER HAMPTON
WITH CONTRIBUTIONS BY AMY POWERS

F C/E Dm7 C/E
Ev-'ry time I see a young kid dream-ing they'll pro-duce a mas-ter-piece
mp
F C/E Dm7 G7 C G/C
BETTY
I just want to throw them on the next train home. Ne-ver thought you'd be so con-de-
C Am/C F C/E Dm7 G7
JOE
-scend-ing. Sor-ry Miss Schae-fer, I did-n't come here to fight.
C G/C C Am/C
BETTY
Girl meets boy, if that's how you want it, she's a young teach-
mf

F C/E Dm7 G7 C
- er, he's a re - port - er, it's hate at first sight.
JOE
Db Ab/Db Db Bm/Db
It won't sell, these days they want gla - mour, fa-bu-lous heir -
mf
Gb Db/F Ebm7 Ab7
- ess meets hand - some Hol - ly-wood heel.
Db Ab7/Db Db Bbm/Db
Prob - lem is she thinks he's a burg - lar. Would you be - lieve

Gb Db/F Ebm7 Ab7
BETTY
— it? A wed - ding in the last reel. It
Gb Db/F Ebm7 Db/F
does-n't have to be so mind-less, you should write from your ex - pe - ri-ence
Gb Db/F Ebm7 Ab
give us some-thing real - ly mo - ving, some - thing true.
JOE
D A/D D Bm/D
Who wants true, who the hell wants mo - ving? Mo-ving means

G D/F♯ Em7 A D A7/D
BETTY
starv-ing and true means holes in your shoe. No, you're wrong, they still make good
D Bm/D G D/F♯
pic - tures, stick to your sto - ry, it's a good
Em7 D/F♯ G6 G/A
JOE
più mosso
Dm(no 3rd)
sto - ry. O. K. Miss Schae-fer, I give it to you.
pp
B♭/D G/D B♭/D
rall.
Dm(no 3rd)

NEW WAYS TO DREAM

MUSIC BY
ANDREW LLOYD WEBBER
LYRICS BY
DON BLACK & CHRISTOPHER HAMPTON

B♭ F G C G C
Mov - ies were born: so ma - ny songs yet to be sung.
B♭ F A♭ G♭ D♭ G
So ma - ny roads still un - ex - plored: we gave the
L.H.
C G Am Dm7/A C/G G7 C
world new ways to dream, some - how we found new ways to dream.
C/G B♭/G F/G G C/G G C/G
Joan of Arc: look at my face, is - n't it strong,

Bb/G F/G G C/G G C
there in the dark, up on the screen where I be - long.
Bb F Ab Gb Db G
We'll show them all no - thing has changed. We'll give the
L.H.
C/G G Am Dm7/A C/G G7 C
world new ways to dream. Ev - 'ry - one needs new ways to dream.
rall.
Bb F Ab Gb Db G C/G G7 C

THE PERFECT YEAR

MUSIC BY
ANDREW LLOYD WEBBER
LYRICS BY
DON BLACK & CHRISTOPHER HAMPTON

B♭m
Dm
Dm/B
F/C
C7
ev-ery-thing I want is here, if you're with me, next year will be the per-fect
F
JOE
F
C7♭9/F
F
year. Be-fore we play some dan-gerous game, be-fore we fan some harm-less
B♭/F
Gm
Gm7
C7
flame, we have to ask if this is wise, and if the game is worth the
F
F7
B♭
B♭m
prize. With this wine, and with this mu - sic, how can a - ny-thing be

Dm
Dm/B
F
C7
F
clear? Let's wait and see, it may just be the per-fect year.
C7/F
F
B♭
Gm
Gm7
C7
F
F7
B♭
B♭m
Dm

F/C
C7
F
accel.
F7
f
B♭
B♭m
Dm
Dm/B
F/C
C7
rit.
D♭
D♭7
NORMA
G♭
D♭7/G♭
It's New Year's Eve, and hopes are high, dance one year
pp
G♭
C♭
A♭m
A♭m7
in, kiss one good - bye, an - oth - er chance, an - oth - er start, so ma - ny

D♭7 G♭ G♭7 C♭
dreams to tease the heart. We don't need a crowd - ed ball - room,
C♭m E♭m A♭7/C G♭/D♭ D♭7
ev-ery-thing we want is here, and face to face we will em - brace the per-fect
G♭ G♭7 C♭ C♭m
year. We don't need a crowd - ed ball - room, ev-ery-thing we want is
E♭m A♭7/C G♭/D♭ ritenuto D♭7 G♭
here, and face to face we will em - brace the per-fect year.

THIS TIME NEXT YEAR

MUSIC BY
ANDREW LLOYD WEBBER
LYRICS BY
DON BLACK & CHRISTOPHER HAMPTON

G
D7
STEVE
next year I'll have land-ed a jui-cy part.
Nine-teen fif-ty will
D7
R. TATE
G
C/G
G
D7
KATE A.
be my start.
No more car-ry-ing spears.
I'll be dis-
G
D7
-co-vered, my life won't ev-er be the same.
G
G7
Bil-ly Wild-er will know my name, and he'll call all the time.

Cmaj7
KATHERINE
Till he does can one of you guys lend her a dime?
Bm/D N.C.
ALISA
D7
Just an a-
mp
G
-part - ment with no roach-es and no dry rot.
D7
ANITA
Where the hot wa - ter
ALISA & ANITA
comes out hot. That's my Hol - ly-wood dream.
G
C/G G D7
RICHARD A.
Your re - so -
G
NADIA
- lu - tion is to write some-thing that gets shot,
D7
with ap - prox - i - mate -

G G7 Cmaj7
MYRON
-ly the plot_ I first had in my head. But you'll get re-writ-ten ev-en
Bm/D D7 G Gm7 C
ARTIE
af - ter you're dead. It's the year to be - gin a new life, buy a
p
D9 D7 Em G2 G
place some-where qui - et, some-where pret - ty. When you have a young
C D Em
kid and a wife, then you need some-where green, far from the ci - ty. It's a

Am7/G D7/G Gmaj7 G6 Am7/G D7/G Gmaj7 G6
ram-bling old house with a big ap-ple tree with a swing for the kid and a ham-mock for me.
PETER
D7 G D7
Be-hold, my child - ren, it is I Ce-cil B. de Mille,
f
mf
meet-ing me must be quite a thrill.
ADAM
G C/G
But there's no need to kneel.
G D7 G D7
PETER
I gua-ran - tee you ev-'ry girl in my cho-rus line

is a ge-nu-ine Phi-li-stine.
SANDY
They don't come off the shelf.
G
Cmaj7 Bm/D D7 G C/G G D7
SAMMY
I flew ev-'ry one in from Phi-lis-tia my-self.
BETTY
I have some
G
good news,
JOE D7
it's 'Blind Win-dows.' You don't let go.
BETTY
I gave Shel-drake an
out-line Joe,
G C G
and he swal-lowed the bait.
JOE
Well Hal-le-

BETTY
D7
-lu - jah. While you've been buy - ing vi - cu - na coats,
I've been mak - ing a lot of notes.
Now there's work we should
G
Cmaj7
JOE
Bm/D N.C.
G6
do. Bet-ty you're for-get-ting that I gave it to you.
G
Gmaj7
C
D
Em
You re-mind me of me long a - go, off the bus full of ig - no-rant am - bi - tion.
mp

G C D7 Em
Thought I'd waltz in-to some stu-di-o and a-chieve o-ver-night re-cog-ni-tion. I've seen
Am7/G D7/G G Am7/G D7/G
too ma-ny op-ti-mists sink-ing like stones, felt them suck all the mar-row clean
G Am7 D7 Gmaj7 G6 C7
BETTY
out of my bones. I love 'Blind
F C7
Win-dows' but I can't write it on my own,_ can't we speak on the

F
ARTIE
C7
te - le - phone? All my even-ings are free. Hey, just a
f
F
C7
BETTY
min - ute, I'm the fel-low who bought the ring._ Ar-tie this is a
F
B♭maj7
busi-ness thing. It's im-por-tant to me, you'll be on lo-ca-tion in
Am/C C7
F
B♭maj7
B♭maj7/C C13
Clinch, Ten - nes - see. Please make this your new year's re-so - lu-tion for
L.H.

F
LADIES
D7
G
me. By this time next year I will get my foot
MEN
By this time next year I will get my foot
D7
in the door. Next year I know I'm going to score
in the door. Next year I know I'm going to score
G
Bm/D
D7
an a - maz - ing suc - cess. Cut to the
an a - maz - ing suc - cess. Cut to the

G
D7
mo - ment when they o - pen the en - ve - lope
pass the sta - tu - ette to Bob Hope,
and it's my name you
G
Am7/G
D7/F♯
hear. We'll be down on our knees outside
p
f
mp cresc. poco a poco

Bm7
G/B
Am7
Grau-man's chi - nese.
Palm prints there on the street,
Grau-man's chi - nese.
Palm prints there on the street,
D7
G
Em/G
G
im - mor - ta - li - ty's neat,
this time next
im - mor - ta - li - ty's neat,
this time next
C
F7
year,
this time next year.
year,
this time next year.

G/D
Em/D
— We'll have no - thing to fear, con - tracts all signed,
— We'll have no - thing to fear, con - tracts all signed,
C/D
Am7/D
G/D
three pic - ture deal, yel - low brick road ca - reer.
three pic - ture deal, yel - low brick road ca - reer.
rall.
C6
Bm/D
D7
G
Hope we're not still say - ing these things this time next year.
Hope we're not still say - ing these things this time next year.

SUNSET BOULEVARD

MUSIC BY
ANDREW LLOYD WEBBER
LYRICS BY
DON BLACK & CHRISTOPHER HAMPTON
WITH CONTRIBUTIONS BY AMY POWERS

E♭
A♭sus4
A♭
C7
fame, want-ed my park - ing space at War - ners.
Fm
D♭
But af-ter a year, a one room hell, a mur-phy bed, a ran-cid
E♭
D♭(♭5)/F
Fm
smell, wall-pa-per peel - ing at the cor - ners.
E♭
B♭/D
Sun - set Bou - le-vard, twist - ing bou - le-vard, se - cre-tive and

B♭m/D♭ Fm♭5 Fm Fm♭5 Fm
rich, a lit-tle sca - ry. Sun - set Bou - le-vard,
E♭ B♭/D B♭m/D♭ Fm
tempt - ing bou - le-vard, wait - ing there to swal - low the un - wa - ry.
D♭
Dreams are not e - nough to win a war, out here they're al - ways keep-ing
E♭ A♭sus4 A♭ C/G C7
score, be-neath the tan the bat-tle ra - ges.

Fm
D♭
Smile a rent-ed smile, fill some-one's glass, kiss some-one's wife, kiss some-one's
E♭sus4
E♭7
D♭/F
Fm
ass, we do what-ev-er pays the wa-ges.
mf
f
Fm2
E♭2
Sun-set Bou-le-vard, head-line bou-le-vard,
B♭/D
B♭m/D♭
Fm♭5
Fm
get-ting here is on-ly the be-gin-ning.

E♭/F
Sun - set Bou - le - vard, jack - pot bou - le - vard,
B♭/F
B♭m/F
Fm
once you've won you have to go on win - ning.
D♭
You think I've sold out? Dead right, I've sold out, I've just been wait - ing
mf
E♭/D♭
Fm2
D♭/F
for the right of - fer, comf - 'ta - ble quart - ers, re - gu - lar ra - tions, twen - ty - four hour
f

Fm2
Db
five star room ser - vice.
And if I'm ho - nest I like the la - dy.
f
mp
mp
Fm
I can't help be - ing touched by her fol - ly.
I'm tread - ing wa - ter,
mp
mp
f
Db
Fm
tak - ing the mo - ney, watch-ing her sun - set.
Well, I'm a wri - ter.
C7
Fm
Db
L. A.'s changed a lot ov - er the years since those brave
mp
mf

E♭
A♭sus4
A♭
C7
gold - rush pi - on - eers came in their crea - ky co-vered wa - gons.
f
Fm
D♭
Far as they could go, end of the line, their dreams were yours, their dreams were
E♭
mine, but in those dreams were hid - den dra - gons.
f
Fm2
E♭2
Sun - set Bou - le - vard, fren - zied bou - le - vard,
mf

B♭/D B♭m/D♭ Fm♭5 Fm
swamped with ev-'ry kind of false e-mo-tion.
f
Fm2 Fm E♭
Sun-set Bou-le-vard, bru-tal bou-le-vard,
mf
B♭/D B♭m/D♭ Fm Fm2 Fm
just like you we'll wind up in the o-cean.
F♯m D/F♯
She was sink-ing fast, I threw a rope, now I have suits and she has
mf

E
Asus4
C♯7
hope, it seemed an e - le - gant so - lu - tion.
F♯m
D
One day this must end, it is - n't real, still I'll en - joy a hear - ty
mf
E
D/F♯
F♯m
meal be - fore to - mor - row's ex - e - cu - tion.
E
Esus4
E
B/D♯
Sun - set Bou - le-vard, ruth - less bou - le-vard, des - ti - na-tion

Bm/D
F♯m♭5
F♯m
F♯m
for the sto-ny heart - ed.
Sun - set Bou - le-vard,
E
Esus4
B/D♯
Bm/D
le - thal bou - le-vard, ev - 'ry-one's for - got - ten how they
F♯m
D(♭5)
D
E
F♯m
start - ed here on Sun - set Bou - le - vard.
D/F♯
N.C.
8va
loco

AS IF WE NEVER SAID GOODBYE

MUSIC BY
ANDREW LLOYD WEBBER
LYRICS BY
DON BLACK & CHRISTOPHER HAMPTON
WITH CONTRIBUTIONS BY AMY POWERS

Moderato

Fm/E♭ E♭ E♭maj7 D♭maj7
ov-er-crowd-ed hall-ways, the at-mos-phere as thrill-ing here as al - ways.
L.H.
A♭/C Fm7
Feel the ear-ly morn-ing mad - ness, feel the ma-gic in the mak - ing. Why,
E♭maj7/B♭ A♭/B♭ E♭
ev-ery-thing's as if we ne - ver said good - bye. I've
mf
E♭maj7 Fm/E♭ E♭
spent so ma-ny morn-ings, just try-ing to re-sist you. I'm trem-bling now, you

E♭maj7 D♭maj7 A♭/C
can't know how I've missed you, missed the fai-ry tale ad-ven-tures in this
Fm7 D♭ A♭/C B♭7
ev-er-spin-ning play-ground. We were young to-geth-er, I'm
E♭maj7 A♭/E♭ E♭
com-ing out of make-up, the light's al-rea-dy burn-ing, not long un-til the
f
E♭maj7 D♭maj7 A♭/C
cam-eras will start turn-ing, and the ear-ly morn-ing mad-ness,

Fm
Ebmaj7/Bb
— and the ma-gic in the mak - ing, yes, ev-ery-thing's as if we
Fm7/Bb
Eb
Gm7
Cm7
Gm7
ne - ver said good - bye. I don't want to be a - lone, that's all in the
Cm7
Bb
Cm
Gm
Cm
past. This world's wait - ed long e - nough, I've come home at
Bb7
Ebmaj7
Ab/Eb
last, and this time will be big - ger, and bright-ter than we knew it.
f assai

Eb Ebmaj7 Dbmaj7
So watch me fly, we all know I can do it. Could I
Ab/C Fm7
stop my hand from shak - ing? Has there ev - er been a mo - ment with so
Db Ab/C Bb7 Ebmaj7
much to live for? The whis-pered con - ver - sa - tions in
p
Fm/Eb Eb Ebmaj7
ov - er-crowd-ed hall - ways, so much to say, not just to - day, but

D♭maj7
A♭/C
al - ways. We'll have ear-ly morn-ing mad - ness, we'll have
Fm
E♭maj7/B♭
A♭6/B♭
ma-gic in the mak - ing, yes, ev-ery-thing's as if we ne - ver said good -
Cm
Cm/A
E♭maj7/B♭
A♭6/B♭
B♭7
E♭
D♭/E♭
- bye, yes, ev-ery-thing's as if we ne - ver said good - bye.
A♭
B♭
E♭
B♭7
A♭/E♭
E♭
We taught the world new ways to dream.
L.H.
f
mp

TOO MUCH IN LOVE TO CARE

MUSIC BY
ANDREW LLOYD WEBBER
LYRICS BY
DON BLACK & CHRISTOPHER HAMPTON

rit.
a tempo
JOE
C7 C7♭9 F Dm7 Gm7 C7 F Dm
for? If you were smart, you would keep on walk-ing out of my life, as
B♭ Csus C7 F Dm7 Gm7 C7 F Dm7
fast as you can. I'm not the one you should pin your hopes on, you're fall-ing for the
Gm7 C7 F/A Am F Am B♭
wrong kind of man. This is cra-zy. You know we should call it a day. Sound ad-vice, great ad-vice,
Gm7 C7 F Dm7 Gm7 C7 F F7
let's throw it a-way. I can't con-trol all the things I'm feel-ing, I have-n't got a

B♭ E♭ B♭ B♭/C C7 F
prayer. If I'm a fool, well, I'm too much in love to care. I
Dmaj7 G6/B D Bm7 G/D A7
knew where I was, I'd giv-en up hope, made friends with dis - il - lu - sion. No -
p
Dmaj7 G6/B D
poco rit.
G/D A7
- one in my life, but I look at you, and now it's all con - fu - sion.
BETTY
con moto
D Dmaj7 Bm7 Em A7
Please can you tell me what's happen-ing? I just don't know a - ny - more.
mp

Bm Bm/G♯ Em7 A7
If this is real, how should I feel? What should I look for?
meno mosso
D Bm7 Em A7 D Bm7 Em7 A7
I thought I had ev - ery-thing I need-ed. My life was set, my dreams were in place.
D Bm7 Em A D Bm Em7 A
My heart could see way in-to the fu-ture. All of that goes when I see your face.
D/F♯ F♯m7 D F♯m7 G Em7 A
I should hate you, there I was, the world in my hand. Can one kiss kiss a-way ev - ery-thing I planned?
3
3
3

D Bm7 Em7 A7 D D7 G
I can't con-trol all the things I'm feel-ing. I'm float-ing in mid - air.
C Gmaj7 G6 Asus A D D7/C F/C Dm7
BETTY & JOE
I know it's wrong, but I'm too much in love to care. I thought I had
Gm/C C7 F Dm Gm C F Dm7
ev-ery-thing I need-ed. My life was set, my dreams were in place. My heart could see
Gm7 C7 F Dm7 Gm7 C7 F Am/E
8va
way in-to the fu-ture. All of that goes when I see your face. This is cra-zy.

Printed and bound in Great Britain by Caligraving Limited

12/02 (46258)

EXCLUSIVE DISTRIBUTORS:

MUSIC SALES LIMITED
8/9 FRITH STREET, LONDON W1V 5TZ, ENGLAND

MUSIC SALES PTY LIMITED
120 ROTHSCHILD AVENUE, ROSEBERY, NSW 2018, AUSTRALIA

ORDER NO. RG10323

MUSIC ARRANGED BY LAURENCE ROMAN AND ROY MOORE
PHOTOGRAPHS BY DAVID COOPER
MUSIC PROCESSED BY BARNES MUSIC ENGRAVING
COVER ARTWORK BY DEWYNTERS LIMITED, LONDON

WORLD PREMIERE AT THE ADELPHI THEATRE, MONDAY JULY 12TH, 1993